At half past eight, Arthur trailed behind his papa through the park, past seller after seller, until he came to his favourite one.

Arthur wanted a balloon.

They had lost their smiles.

Papa. Even Arthur.

And balloons made
Arthur smile.

'Today, Papa? Please? The sunny yellow one?
We can take it to the hospital. Mama loves yellow.'

ARTHUR Wants a

BALLOON

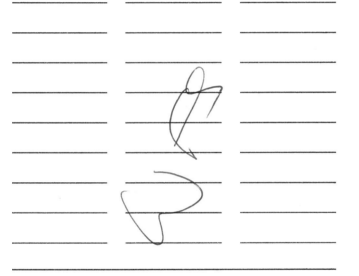

by ELIZABETH GILBERT BEDIA   illustrated by ERIKA MEZA

UPS!DE DOWN BOOKS

Sadness filled
Papa's eyes.

'No, Arthur. We
need to hurry.
Besides, the
blustery clouds
will whisk it away.'

Arthur gazed up.

The clouds let out
a gloomy sigh.

So did Papa.

And so did Arthur.

The next day, Arthur hurried behind his papa through the park.

'Today, Papa?' asked Arthur. 'The bright red one like the bird in the tree?'

'Not today, Arthur. We're going to be late. Besides, it's not a day for balloons.'

Arthur scowled at the sky.
The clouds drooped.

As did Papa.

And Arthur.

The following day, Arthur was afraid to look.

Raindrops **plip-plopped** on his nose.

Arthur plodded behind
his papa as the rain fell.

Then, Arthur saw the brilliant bundle waving at him.
He spotted the perfect balloon.

'Can I have the bright blue one like the splishy-splashy puddles?
Please, Papa? It's your favourite colour!'

A glimmer appeared in Papa's eyes,
but it disappeared just as quickly.

Papa hurried on as
usual, and the rain
fell faster and faster.

Drip,
drop,
drip.

'No, Arthur.'

Drip,
drop,
drip.

Drip,
drop,
drip.

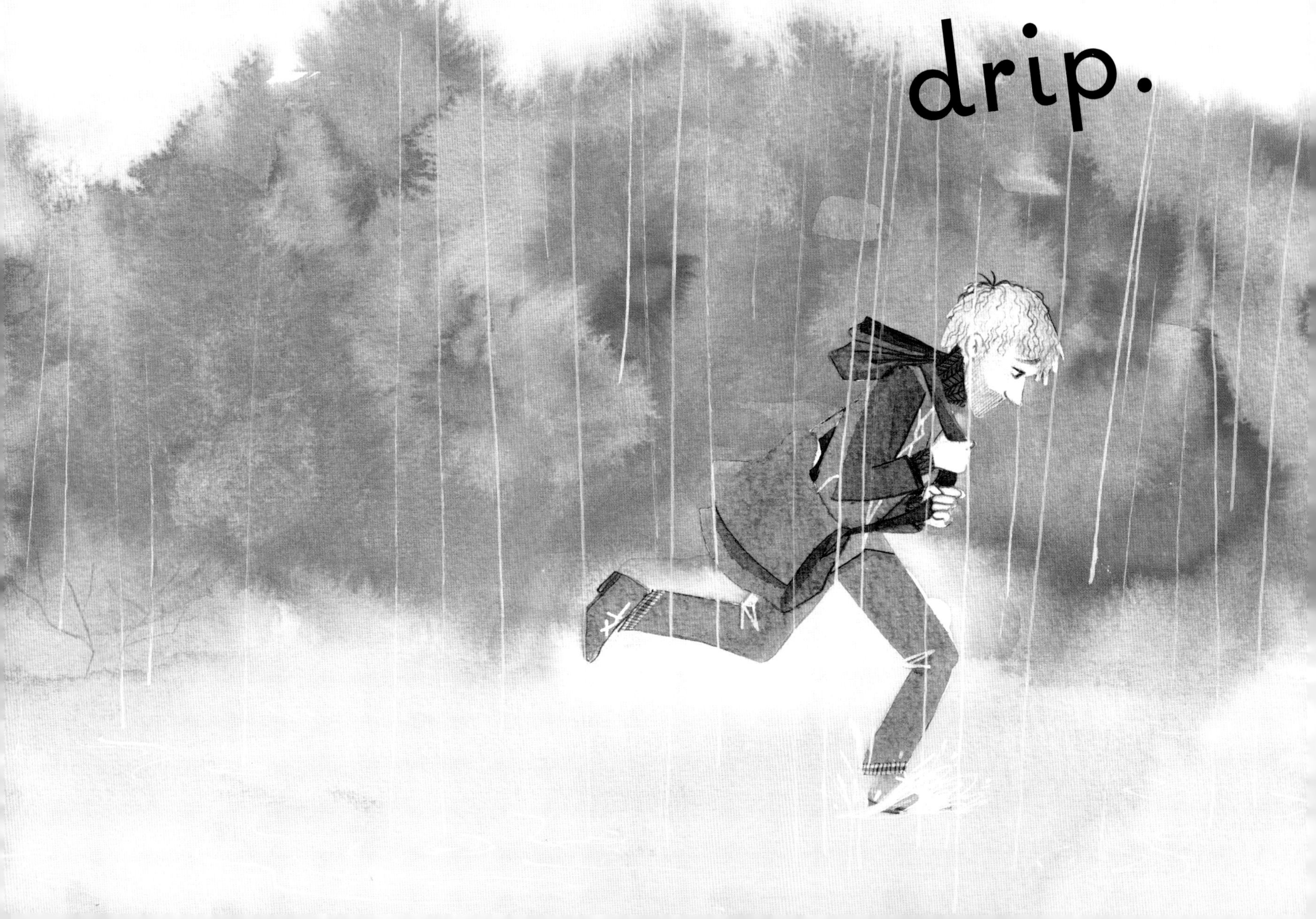

Why is Papa being this way? wondered Arthur,
as his tears fell as fast as the rain.

The clouds burst open with a downpour.

Arthur gazed up at them. 'Are you sad, too?'

That night, Arthur dreamed of a bundle of balloons
and Mama smiling back at him.

But then ...

... the clouds covered
them all.

At eight o'clock, he
dashed down the stairs
and out the door,
then stopped.

To his surprise ...

Arthur awoke more determined
than ever.

... a bundle of balloons was stuck in the tree right outside the house!

'Look, Papa, look!'

'I wonder how
they got here?'
Papa said.

Papa helped
Arthur up to
the balloons.

Arthur held the strings
tightly in one hand

and held out his
other hand ...

... to **Papa.**

At that moment, Arthur realised
what he really wanted.

'Arthur, I thought you wanted the balloons,' said Papa.

'I thought I did, too,' said Arthur.

'But?'

'**You** need them more,' said Arthur.

'And **SO** does Mama.'

For the first time in a long time, Papa smiled.

'Oh, Arthur. You found my smile.'

Then, Arthur
smiled too.

'Hurry, Papa! Mama is waiting for us.'

For Erik, Jacob and Grace, whose generous smiles chase away the clouds. – E.G.B.

To Paul, who - through thick mists and sunny days - reminds me to look up to the sky. – E.M.

UPSIDE DOWN BOOKS

First published in Great Britain 2020 by Upside Down Books
an imprint of Trigger Publishing

Trigger Publishing is a trading style of
Shaw Callaghan Ltd & Shaw Callaghan 23 USA, INC.
The Foundation Centre
Navigation House, 48 Millgate, Newark
Nottinghamshire NG24 4TS UK
www.triggerpublishing.com

British Library Cataloguing in Publication Data

A CIP catalogue record for this book is available upon request
from the British Library
ISBN: 978-1-78956-116-6
EPUB: 978-1-78956-167-8
KF8: 978-1-78956-233-0

Elizabeth Gilbert Bedia and Erika Meza have asserted their rights under the
Copyright, Design and Patents Act 1988 to be identified as the author of this work

Designed by Kathryn Davies
Printed and bound in China
Paper from responsible sources

for mama

It is important for children to understand their own emotional state, as well as the emotional states of others. Building sympathy and empathy from a young age are keys to positive mental health. And wanting to help those in need is a natural human response—especially within children. *Arthur Wants a Balloon* brings young readers empathy in abundance, as a poignant story about a little boy trying to understand his father's gloomy mood and wanting to help. This insightful book promotes kindness and compassion, especially in the wake of depression. It is a must-read for children whose parents experience mental health challenges.

Lauren Callaghan

Consultant Clinical Psychologist,
Co-founder and Clinical Director of Trigger Publishing